HOW TO
SAVE YOUR
MARRIAGE
ALONE

HOW TO SAVE YOUR MARRIAGE ALONE

Ed Wheat, M.D.

ZONDERVAN PUBLISHING HOUSE
OF THE ZONDERVAN CORPORATION
GRAND RAPIDS, MICHIGAN 49506

HOW TO SAVE YOUR MARRIAGE ALONE
Copyright © 1983 by The Zondervan Corporation
Grand Rapids, Michigan

This book consists of two chapters taken from the larger book, *Love Life for Every Married Couple,* copyright © 1980 by Ed Wheat, M.D.

Unless otherwise indicated Scripture references are taken from the King James Version of the Bible. Other versions include:

The Amplified Bible. Copyright © 1965 by The Zondervan Corporation. Used by permission.
New American Standard Bible. Copyright © 1972 by The Lockman Foundation, Creation House, Carol Stream, Illinois. Used by permission.

Library of Congress Cataloging in Publication Data

Wheat, Ed.
    How to save your marriage alone.

    Two chapters from: Love life for every married couple. c1980.
    Bibliography: p.
    1. Marriage.   2. Marriage—Religious aspects—Christianity.
3. Love.   4. Christian life.   5. Sex in marriage.   I. Title.
HQ734.W52325   1983   306.8'1   83-10302
ISBN 0-310-42522-0

Printed in the United States of America

83 84 85 86 87 88 / 9 8 7 6 5 4 3 2 1

Contents

Husbands, love your wives, even as Christ also loved the church, and gave himself for it;

That he might sanctify and cleanse it with the washing of water by the word,

That he might present it to himself a glorious church, not having spot, or wrinkle, or any such thing; but that it should be holy and without blemish.

So ought men to love their wives as their own bodies. He that loveth his wife loveth himself.

For no man ever yet hated his own flesh; but nourisheth and cherisheth it, even as the Lord the church:

For we are members of his body, of his flesh, and of his bones.

For this cause shall a man leave his father and mother, and shall be joined unto his wife, and they two shall be one flesh.

This is a great mystery: but I speak concerning Christ and the church.

Nevertheless let every one of you in particular so love his wife even as himself; and the wife see that she reverence her husband.

(Ephesians 5:25–33)

1

How to Save Your Marriage Alone

This chapter is directed to a special group of readers: those individuals who want to save their marriage at all costs, even though they have to do it alone without any help from their partner. In fact, their partner may be actively pursuing a divorce.

If you are in this group, I do indeed consider you *special*. First, by your stand you indicate a commitment to the sacredness and permanence of marriage that is God-honoring; second, you have the courage to face your own problems instead of running from them or hiding behind false pride; and, third, you exhibit the maturity which, even when there is no response, can choose to love with a steadfast love that is tough and real, intelligent and purposeful, wholly committed to your partner's well-being.

Christian psychiatrist Paul D. Meier says that there are "only three choices for any person involved in an unhappy marriage: (1) get a divorce—the greatest cop-out and by far the most immature choice; (2) tough out the marriage without working to improve it—another immature decision but not quite as irresponsible as divorce; and (3) maturely face up to personal hangups and choose to build an intimate marriage out of the existing one—the only really mature choice to make."[1]

In your case, the moment of truth has come, for your partner probably has already ruled out the second option and chosen the first without even considering the third. The question is, What will *you* do? Surrender to the pressures of the world's way of thinking and the emotions of the moment? Or make a choice based on confidence in the eternal truths of Scripture?

The stakes are higher than one may realize at the time. One choice clearly leads to the bitterness and defeat of divorce as well as lost opportunities for blessing. "Divorce is more painful than death," a women told me the other day, her voice husky with pent-up emotion, *"because it's never really over."* Dr. Meier says that when couples run away from their problems by divorcing and remarrying, "then there are four miserable people instead of just two. . . . Why spread misery?" he asks. "Bad marriages are contagious! Numerous psychiatric research studies have shown that when couples with neurotic marriage relationships get divorced—no matter how good their intentions may be—they nearly always remarry into the very same type of neurotic relationship they had before."[2]

When you choose the pathway of irrevocable commitment to your mate and your marriage—regardless of how troubled your relationship may seem—you will find that choice leading you into a place of *agape* love and peace and personal growth. These are just some of the rewards, for the chances are very good that you will also be able to enjoy the blessings that God has wanted to bestow on your marriage from the beginning.

I am not suggesting that the healing of a marriage is an easy process when one partner resists it. But are any easy choices open to you, after all? Torn relationships involve pain, whatever you do about them. As Peter points out in his first letter, it is far better to suffer (if suffer you must) for doing *right,* than for doing wrong. He makes it clear that God's favor and blessing shine on the one who patiently suffers, if necessary, in order to do His will. Meeting your marriage problems in a biblical manner is productive rather than pointless, and whatever hurts you encounter will be less damaging than the long-term effects of divorce would be.

"The very word *divorce* should be cut out of the vocabulary of a couple when they marry," a woman with a restored marriage said, "because God's way is so much better for anyone who is willing to give it a try."

Another woman, considering the turbulent events of the past year that had driven her to grow emotionally and spiritually while she "loved her husband back" to their marriage, said, "You know, it's been all gain for me. I'm a different person now. The process was humbling, but it was worth it!"

A man said, "During the time when I was trying to win my wife's love and hold our family together, sometimes I got so tired of rejection that I didn't feel anything except a determination to do what the Bible said and leave the results with God. The only thing I was sure of was that somehow God would work it out for my good because He promised that in His Word. I never imagined the love affair He has actually given us. He really does do more than we can ask or think!"

While these comments from the far side of the problem are encouraging, I understand that the feelings you may be experiencing right now within the problem are less than pleasant. Many others have been where you are now and can empathize with what you are going through: shock, hurt, rejection, emotional confusion, temptation to bitterness, and, of course, pressures from all sides that sometimes make you want to give up.

My heartfelt goal in this chapter is to help you clarify your thoughts, stabilize your emotions, and learn to behave in a consistent, purposeful way that will save your marriage and bring a new dimension of love into your relationship.

So, if you are willing to make a commitment to your marriage based on the eternal principles and promises of the Word of God, you can take heart and let hope grow in proportion to your commitment. Contrary to what the world believes, one person *can* save a marriage. In fact, most of the people I counsel belong in this category. Even when both come to see me, one is usually dragging the other along, in a manner of speaking, and only one really cares about the outcome in most cases.

Marriage counselor Anne Kristin Carroll says, "If you think there's no hope because you are the only one in your relationship who wants or cares enough to try to save your marriage, you are wrong!" She adds, "In my experience most torn marriages are brought to new life, new vitality, by the interest, basically, of only one party."[3] This has been my experience as well. I have seen numerous marriages saved when only one partner applied biblical principles in a wholehearted commitment to the mate and the marriage.

Some have not been saved. Usually this is because the individual is convinced that nothing will change the partner—that the longstanding problem of alcoholism or financial irresponsibility or whatever cannot be solved, and he or she simply gives up. Occasionally, the partner desiring a divorce has developed such a strong emotional attachment to another person that it is not broken off *in time* to save the marriage. Often, however, this infatuation ends while the divorce is being delayed, and the unfaithful partner thanks the committed mate for standing fast and preserving the marriage. In a relatively few cases, one partner pressured by family and "loyal" friends, develops a deep bitterness toward the other and is actually encouraged in this hostility by parents and even, sometimes, church members so that efforts at reconciliation may be unavailing.

But in the great majority of cases, the outcome depends squarely on the committed partner's ability to behave consistently in accord with biblical principles designed by the Author of marriage. So, in a very literal sense, it is *all* up to you. You need not expect your partner to do anything constructive about the marriage if he or she wants out.

Clarifying Your Thoughts

When the Bible says, "Gird up the loins of your mind" (1 Peter 1:13), it means to get your mental powers in a state of alertness for proper action. You must do this without delay. Often the Lord will provide the opportunity for some quiet, uninterrupted Bible study and prayerful consideration of God's plan for your situation. You may also learn some important things about yourself during this time. When one husband moved out, his parents lovingly helped the wife by keeping the children for several weeks while she prepared mentally and spiritually for the challenges ahead.

One young wife was ready to dissolve her marriage until a friend in her garden club led her to the Lord. "I only knew two Scriptures at the beginning," the wife said, "but they were exactly what I needed: 'God is not a man, that he should lie' (Numbers 23:19) and 'With God nothing shall be impossible' (Luke 1:37).

"With those truths as a foundation I began to study the Bible, desperately trying to dig out God's purpose for marriage and all that He had to say about it. I found out for myself that if I were to obey Him, then I would have to become committed to my marriage and my husband, even though he was involved with another woman and we were on the verge of divorce.

"Coming to this decision didn't make things any easier emotionally at first, but it did show me a clear path of action, and the situation actually became less complicated because there was no more confusion about *what* to do! I refused to sign the divorce papers. I had gathered evidence identifying the other woman and proving my husband's unfaithfulness. I destroyed it all. I didn't need it anymore.''

A University of Chicago professor described this generation's dilemma with the now familiar quotation: "We lack the *language* to teach what is right and wrong." But the Bible-believing Christian caught in an emotionally fraught situation does not have that problem. The language of God concerning divorce is plain enough for any reader. For example:

> For the Lord, the God of Israel, says: I hate divorce and marital separation, and him who covers his garment [his wife] with violence. Therefore keep a watch upon your spirit [that it may be controlled by My Spirit], that you deal not treacherously and faithlessly [with your marriage mate] (Malachi 2:16 AMPLIFIED).

> He replied, Have you never read that He Who made them from the beginning made them male and female. And said, For this reason a man shall leave his father and mother and shall be united firmly (joined inseparably) to his wife, and the two shall become one flesh? So they are no longer two but one flesh. What therefore God has joined together, let not man put asunder (separate) (Matthew 19:4–6 AMPLIFIED).

As you try to gain clarity of thought concerning your marital situation viewed in light of the teaching of Scripture, I suggest that you read my book *Love Life for Every Married Couple* and *search the Scriptures* that have to do with marriage. Let me remind you once more of the eternal principle that undergirds the biblical counsel we offer: *It is God's will in every marriage for the couple to love each other with an absorbing spiritual, emotional, and physical attraction that continues to grow throughout their lifetime together*. It should be crystal clear that God intends for you and your mate to picture the love-bond of Christ and His church and that you must beware of substitutes who sometimes find their way into the vacuum of a troubled relationship. Obviously, infidelity and divorce are paths that move away from God's plan and blessing. But when you pour yourself into restoring love to your marriage, you can be sure that the force of His will is at work with you in the process.

It is important to fill your mind with positive biblical input: biblical counseling, preaching, and teaching; good books and Bible-study tapes; and friends who will affirm you in your commitment to your marriage. You need to take in truth from those who are as committed to the permanence of marriage as the Bible is. And don't listen to anyone else! Develop tunnel vision in this area as Proverbs 4:25–27 commands:

> Let your eyes look directly ahead, and let your gaze be fixed straight in front of you. Watch the path of your feet, and all your ways will be established. Do not turn to the right nor to the left; turn your foot from evil (NASB).

You need to maintain this total mental commitment to the truth or you will be swamped by waves of human opinion and bad advice, sometimes from seemingly religious people.

One young man came to me, confused because he had been told to do nothing to win back his wife. He had been told to concentrate on his vertical relationship with God. I said to him, "This is true, but you can please God only when you are doing what the Bible says you are to do. You must be right in line with God's Word. We have no other direction for this life. When we are in total accord with the Word, then we can relax and God has the freedom to work with us. He always works with us on the basis of the information that we have from His Word. So the more you know of the Word of God concerning marriage and love and His abhorrence of divorce, the more equipped you will be to let God do His full work and have His full way in your life.''

"I had to take a stand on this matter of outside influence," a wife told me. "Everyone has been anxious to give me advice about my marriage. I refuse to discuss it with people who hold an unbiblical viewpoint, or people who try to turn me against my husband, or people who make me feel sorry for myself and encourage weakness in me. I can't afford to be around worldly friends anymore. They tear me down; they tear my husband down. They may mean well, but they are so misguided. I want to be with people who will stand with me and support me when I might falter.''

When your mind is settled, your thoughts clarified, and your commitment made, you will find that you no longer lie at the mercy of outside events, reacting to every new circumstance with fresh pain and bewilderment. Instead, your viewpoint becomes, "This is what I am going to do, *no matter what*, because it is God's way to do it. I can count on His wisdom, and I can trust Him with the results of a course of action based on His Word.''

"I'm not standing by my marriage anymore on the basis of what the outcome will be," one woman told me. "People urge me to dump my husband, give up on him because he's made my life miserable; they tell me I deserve someone better, that I wouldn't have any trouble finding someone else to love me. My answer is that marriage is sacred; marriage is permanent; I am committed by my marriage vows; I am one flesh with my husband; and then I really shock them! I tell them that even if there is no happy ending for our marriage, I will not regret the stand I have taken. I will know that I made the right decision and followed the only course possible for me. I will have done all that I could.

"But my trust is not in what I am doing," she added. "It is

14

in God and His Word. He has a perfect, loving plan for my life, and He's wise enough and powerful enough to carry it out, if I cooperate by following His counsel. So I'm going to keep on obeying Him in my marriage and I'll leave the results with Him. I am at peace with that.''

Stabilizing Your Emotions

As a medical doctor I often know when a marriage is in trouble because my patients come to me for something to alleviate their highly nervous state. One wife whose husband was intensely infatuated with someone else came to me convinced that she was on the verge of ''losing her mind.'' She feared that she might not survive and had pleaded with her in-laws to keep her children away from contact with the other woman if something happened to her. Her mental anguish was indeed acute.

Months later I was impressed by the transformation in this woman—alert, poised, attractive, well-balanced in thought and speech, she now seemed to possess a central core of peace. Although her marital problems were not completely resolved, her husband had returned home and they were working together to build a real love relationship.

''Before he could tell me he loved me, even before he came back home, he was impressed with how I had changed,'' she explained. ''He was in such a turmoil, and the peace and stability that I had found really attracted him to me.'' She opened her Bible. ''Did you know that Proverbs 5:6 says an adulteress's ways are *unstable?* My husband found that out! The contrast with the spiritual maturity that I had gained the hard way inspired his respect and made him want to be with me.''

''How do you account for this change in you?'' I asked, although I was sure I already knew the answer.

15

"The Lord changed me through the Word of God," she said. "It was as if I were drowning, and the Word was the lifeline. I spent hours every day in the Bible. To begin with, the Lord showed me how wrong I had been as a wife. I couldn't feel betrayed and mistreated anymore; I couldn't even blame my husband for looking for someone else to make him happy when I had failed so badly. I saw that I had to change, and the Word showed me how.

"Then the Lord showed me that I couldn't be bitter toward the other woman. Bitterness was out. Love was in. And all the time the promises of the Word of God were stabilizing me, giving me a steadiness to face each new day. When something occurred that seemed like a severe setback, I could calmly go to the Word and study and begin to understand the new lesson He was teaching me.

"As *you* know," she said, "when this all started, I just had to have someone I could call day or night to talk to because I was so scared, so hurt, so desperate. But the time came when I learned to go straight to the Lord. It took a while to reach that, but it's the greatest blessing for me out of this whole experience. I've learned that all I really need is the Lord!"

This wife's testimony points the way to emotional stability for any individual who needs it—and most people faced with the disintegration of their marriage desperately need it.

In a magazine article, "Fly by the Instruments," Gloria Okes Perkins compares times of trial and emotional instability in the believer's life with the clouds, fog, and air turbulence an airplane pilot experiences. The answer in both cases is to fly entirely by the instruments.

"When there is no visual contact with the earth . . . when no horizon is in view, stability can be achieved only by depending on what those vital gyros have to say," she writes. "What is true for pilots in the skies is just as true in another sense for believers in the difficulties of life when normal conditions of stability seem to vanish in clouds of sorrow and confusion. Sooner or later every believer will have to 'fly by instruments' spiritually and emotionally through bad times. . . .

"While piloting a plane in a thick fog, a pilot cannot be sure of his direction unless he gives full attention to his instruments. When flying through a thunderstorm, the turbulence will throw him about, and the darkness within the clouds will threaten to disorient him. Sometimes he will feel as though he is going up or down or turning around. But he cannot depend on his feelings. Only the gyros can be trusted, so the pilot must hang on to the controls in the turbulence and discipline his mind to concentrate on the instruments while he flies through the storm.

"The parallel truth for the Christian in troubled times is clear. Undisciplined feelings . . . can cause a crash unless one keeps himself stabilized by the facts of the Word of God. . . . Every promise in the Word of God is like a gyro giving information to stabilize him in a specific situation. . . . With daily practice one learns not to panic but to believe a specific truth from the Bible fitted for his own unique circumstances. By experience one learns not to fight his feelings, but to look away from them to the 'instrument panel' of the Word of God which is utterly dependable.

"One discovers that if he will just hang on in the worst of the turbulence, no matter how disrupting, his mind and heart steadied by the great truths of the Word and his eyes intently fixed on God Himself, He will eventually break through rain-black clouds to soar once more in the clear, tranquil atmosphere."[4]

This is the way *you* can gain emotional stability at this time, no matter what your situation.

Learning to Love

We come now to the practical behavior that can save your marriage. Your challenge is to learn how to love your partner day in and day out in such a way that there will be a responding love. Remember, you become loveable by loving, not by straining to attract love. So be careful how you love. Loving your mate in God's way does not mean clinging, complaining, or making demands. Moodiness, anger, and temperamental displays will only hinder your efforts. Loving your mate in God's way does not mean playing games—trying to inspire jealousy or insecurity, playing hard to get, taking petty revenge, or any of the other approaches you may have used in your early teens that are wholly inappropriate for marriage.

I recommend that you read 1 Corinthians 13, in as many different modern English translations as you can find. Read it again and again to learn the behavior patterns that characterize the genuine loving that God can use in healing a marriage. Fill your mind and spirit with these basic behavior responses so that they can reshape your attitudes and change your actions.

One wife asked her husband, "What can I do to show you that I love you?" This was his answer: "You could be nice to me all of the time, not just when you're in the mood. You could treat me as if I were really special. You could show me that you love me by respecting me and not trying to take over."

A wife expressed her desire in this way: "I just want my husband to keep telling me that he loves me and approves of me. Not only with words but also with kisses and thoughtfulness and understanding and protectiveness. I suppose what I'm really saying is that I want him to love me the way the Bible says—to love me the way Jesus Christ loves the church!"

We all hunger to be loved. And we want tangible proof that we *are* loved. But someone in the marriage has to take the initiative and begin the loving process. When misunderstandings piled upon misunderstandings erect walls between husband and wife, this can be difficult. Robert Louis Stevenson spoke the truth when he said, "Here we are, most of us, sitting at the window of our heart, crying for someone to come in and love us. But then we cover up the window with the stained glass of pride or anger or self-pity so that no one can glimpse the lonely self inside."

Is it possible in your own marriage that two lonely people are crying out for love on the inside, yet confused about what the other really wants and feels? There is only one constructive answer. You must choose to love your partner, unilaterally at first, and show it by meeting not only his or her needs, but desires as well.

In short, you will need to apply all the principles discussed in my book *Love Life for Every Married Couple* concerning the five ways of loving and how to love. The easiest way to establish an effective habit of loving behavior is to follow the B-E-S-T prescription of chapter 13 of that book.

At one of our Christian marriage seminars in the South, a middle-aged couple came up to Gaye and me, smiling broadly and obviously happy. The wife's first words were, "We just wanted to meet the people responsible for the *Love-Life* cassette album that saved our marriage!" Taking turns, their faces radiant, they explained how they had given up on their marriage with their relationship problems seemingly insurmountable. But then a Christian counselor gave them our *Love-Life* cassette album, and they found hope for the first time. They had carefully followed our suggestions step by step and discovered that they worked. The wife reached in her purse, pulled out her billfold, and took a card out to show us. On it she had outlined the B-E-S-T prescription with a few lines under each point. She said, "I used to look at this many times in the course of a day, and I still use it daily to remind me how to love. Our marriage is so good now—I do not want to slip back into the old patterns of behavior that almost destroyed it!''

Loving your partner by blessing, edifying, sharing, and touching should become a lifetime habit. Not only does it inspire a responding love, but it will bring to life your own feelings of love and keep them alive. This occurs because feelings are determined by actions—not the other way around. If you behave as if you love someone, the *feelings* will inevitably follow in a short time. And by behaving in a positive way through the B-E-S-T plan, you can avoid the emotional numbness you would otherwise develop as a result of your mate's continued rejection.

Even while applying all the rest of the counsel in this book, if you alone are trying to save your marriage you are in a special situation that demands special measures and additional counsel. For, how can you show love when your partner is occupied with someone else? Or has moved out of the home? Or meets your love with hostility? Or totally ignores you?

The special advice I have for you will run counter to everything the worldly mind teaches, and it will go against your own nature to do it. But if you want to save your marriage, you cannot afford to indulge your pride or exalt yourself. You will not even be able to carry out this counsel on your own because only the individual with spiritual resources through a knowledge of the written Word of God and the abiding presence of the Lord Jesus Christ can consistently and effectively do what needs to be done.

The spiritual principle you must comprehend and lay hold of is this: ''He (the Lord) has said to me, 'My grace is sufficient for you, for power is perfected in weakness.' Most gladly, therefore, I will rather boast about my weaknesses, that the

20

power of Christ may dwell in me . . . for when I am weak, then I am strong" (2 Corinthians 12:9–10b NASB).

In the light of that principle, which operates in the Christian's life whenever applied, here is preparation you need to make in your purposeful effort to save your marriage.

1) Prepare for the worst, knowing you have a sufficiency of grace.

Usually when a troubled relationship exists, the mate who wants to leave either is involved with another person or anticipates involvement with someone else. So, when a person comes to me with a marriage problem, one of the first things I ask is this:

"Is your partner involved with someone else?"

Often the answer is a reluctant, "Yes, somewhat. . . ."

"All right," I say, "what would you do if your mate were involved in adultery with that person?"

"Well," the individual may say, "it hasn't gone that far yet!"

Then I explain that he or she must be prepared to face the possibility. One wife clung to the belief that her husband (an active Christian) could not possibly have gone as far as the act of adultery with the other woman (a Christian "friend"). When the truth came out, it was doubly devastating because she was totally unprepared to handle it.

Another wife began to prepare emotionally and spiritually for the possibility of her husband's unfaithfulness as a result of Gaye's counsel to her at a seminar. The wife called later to tell us that her husband had come to her soon after the seminar with a confession: he had had a lengthy affair with his secretary. "I'm so glad I was prepared," the wife told us. "He wanted to stay with me, but he thought it would be hopeless once I knew the truth about his past. I had been listening to the

21

Love-Life cassettes over and over again, and I was able to handle the situation with calmness and love and forgiveness. I already had my mind focused on the important thing—saving our marriage. We're going to do it.''

Adultery probably is the worst sin that most mates can think of their partner committing. It is wise to be prepared practically, emotionally, and spiritually for the worst. Then other problems will become easier to handle if they are ''all'' you have to contend with. Prepare for the possibility of infidelity by realizing that adultery is sin—the same as any other sin, because God can forgive that individual and so can you! You must forgive if you are to be free to love and live and grow as a person.

Karen Mains, in *The Key to a Loving Heart*, vividly describes the connection between forgiveness and love:

> The key that opens the door to the locked rooms of our hearts is forgiveness. It is only when we have experienced forgiveness (. . . I mean being overwhelmed by the reality of forgiveness, being able to touch, taste, and smell its results) that we find the locks are sprung, the doors flung open, the windows tossed high, the rooms inhabited, the fires lighted on the hearths. It is then we discover that our hearts are finally free to love. They have become what the Creator intended them to be, places with immense capacity to embrace.

After you have forgiven, you must prepare yourself to cope with a continuation of the affair and decide exactly how you will handle it, even rehearsing in your mind how you will respond to certain situations that might arise. You must be prepared to respond in a loving way, even to a continuing infidelity. It's not that you are condoning it; it's not that you are ignoring it. But early on in the process of resolving your marriage problems you have to come to the powerful realization that *you* cannot reform your mate, no matter how hard you try. Your only option is to become the husband or wife God has commanded you to be in Scripture, and to apply every principle of behavior from the Word of God to the day-by-day challenges of your situation. You may well save your marriage. Without question, you will enjoy God's blessing and favor.

What will change your mate? Sometimes the change comes through a personal knowledge of the Scriptures. One Christian husband forsook his adulterous affair and came home because through personal Bible reading he realized how deeply he had fallen into sin and how terrible the results of that could be. His wife told me, "I thought he had come home because he loved me. But he admitted that he came back in obedience to God's Word. That really did something to my pride at first! My husband said, 'God promises me that He will teach me how to love you as you should be loved.' Then I realized how dumb I had been with my hurt pride. I should be thanking the Lord because this is the best way for us to begin building a real love relationship. If he had come back just because I looked more attractive to him at the moment, it wouldn't have lasted. Now, with *both* of us, our strength and hope to rebuild our marriage rests with the Lord."

But what about the mate who will not go to the Word of God for counsel? In that case, he or she must see in you a living, walking example of God's truth being applied faithfully in every situation. Never leave the impression that you are behaving this way just to change your mate. You do it because God said that you must, whether it seems to work or not.

In severely troubled marriages, it is usually the husband who comes and goes from the family home, perhaps spending part of the time with another woman. While this is obviously distasteful, I sometimes counsel wives to accept this situation on a temporary basis as it is preferable to total separation leading to dissolution of the marriage.

For this reason, your husband is given the freedom to be in both worlds for a time while he tries to live out his fantasy. If you are doing your part at home, a clear contrast will become evident to him. "The lips of an adulteress drip honey, and smoother than oil is her speech; But in the end she is bitter as wormwood, sharp as a two-edged sword. Her feet go down to death. . . . She does not ponder the path of life; her ways are unstable, she does not know it" (Proverbs 5:3–6 NASB). Sooner or later, this will become apparent to your husband. You have the opportunity, if he is still coming home at least part of the time, to show him genuine sweetness with no bitter aftertaste and the gracious, stable serenity that only Christ can give. Your behavior can remind him of the continuing joy and dignity of remaining as the head of his family in contrast to the social, spiritual degradation that biblically is promised to the man who casts his lot with an adulteress. You will not accomplish this by trying, but by *being*: being the loving, gracious wife God would have you to be as defined in the Scriptures.

This is why I urge all men and women under my counseling to avoid separation no matter how serious their problems are. (The only exception is in the case of actual physical injury that could require a legal separation.) As long as the two of you live in the same household, you have the daily opportunity to put powerful biblical principles into action. Don't underestimate your advantage. You are in a position to love so unchangingly that the impact on your partner will intensify with the passing of time. As you consistently apply eternal concepts to your daily relationship, time and togetherness become your helpers in restoring love to your marriage. If you are living apart, then you must take advantage of every common bond you have, such as children or business, to display love through your behavior and attitudes.

The rule is to show him the difference when he is home;

make him glad to be there! One wife described how she behaved toward her husband who was beset by financial problems and wavering between home and the other woman's apartment. "I was willing to let my husband have what we had accumulated (mostly debts)," she smiled. "But the other woman was pressuring him to leave home and telling him what she would allow him to give to his children. I thought, He's got one woman pressuring him. He doesn't need two. So I left him alone, coped without demanding money from him, and refused to charge to his accounts. Originally, in his own thinking, he had placed me in the middle of his financial problems while the other woman represented freedom to him—the fantasy of starting over unhindered. But that soon changed. He saw I was on his side—concerned about him, and trusting the Lord to provide for the children and me financially. In contrast, she was demanding expensive furniture and clothes from the best shops. Yes, it hurt to go without a new coat and see her sport a $250 model. But I had to laugh. I knew it wouldn't last long. And it didn't. He's home now—permanently. Our marriage is on a new, solid footing."

In preparing to face the worst that could assault your marriage, you must remember that people ensnared by infatuation and involved in an extramarital affair are suffering from a kind of temporary insanity. They are not thinking clearly: they may behave in totally irresponsible ways; they seem beyond the reach of normal judgment. You will have to realize that this does occur. Even this has to be accepted and dealt with in your own emotional preparation. As one wife said, "While my husband was 'out of it' I didn't try to reason with him. I didn't condemn or judge or scorn or rebuke. I just accepted him the way he was. During that period, I used the waiting time to grow in the Lord myself. Happily, my husband is back to normal now and a lot wiser than before."

When the wife in the marriage becomes infatuated with someone else she will usually move out of the home permanently or demand that her husband leave the home. I counsel the husband not to move away. There is no way he can be forced out of his home if his behavior is moderate and reasonable.

Husbands must be prepared to actively pursue their wives and win them back. But the wife should never be allowed to feel that he is doing this out of duty. Only love will have the force to prevail over the warring emotions that have brought an unfaithful wife to this point.

For instance, a church-going wife's one-time indiscretion became public knowledge. Deeply ashamed and emotionally confused, she left her husband and moved into an apartment where, in a combination of guilt, defiance, and loneliness, she continued to see the other man. Her husband had all the sympathy from their family and church friends. But was he blameless in the matter? Or had he failed to love her as he should before the act of infidelity occurred? In almost every case, the injured party has to bear some responsibility for the breakdown of the marriage. In this situation, the wife's out-of-character behavior had developed after the tragic loss of their child. The husband recognized that he perhaps had failed to exhibit the sensitive understanding he should have shown her at that time. Clearly, he had failed to meet her needs and desires.

Now he had a choice. He could let her go or he could win her back (as did Hosea in the Old Testament), restoring her to her former place of honor. I reminded him of two scriptural principles from Ephesians 5. First, he and that girl were intimately united whether they were living apart or together. As the church is Christ's body, so the wife is, in a sense, the husband's body. Public opinion and her temporary indiscretions and foolish behavior could not change that eternal fact. Second, "He who loves his own wife loves himself; for no one ever hated his own flesh, but nourishes and cherishes it" (Ephesians 5:28–29 NASB).

I counseled this husband to love his wife back to their marriage by nourishing her emotionally and cherishing her in every possible way during this upheaval in her life. "If you approach her as though you are being noble and doing her a favor, you will get nowhere," I warned. "You have to convince her that you love her, that she is valuable and precious beyond any other woman in your sight, that you need her and do not want to live without her."

Another husband had been told by Christian friends to pray and ask God to bring his wife back, then to do nothing, trusting God to work in some supernatural way.

"But your marriage relationship is to picture the relationship between Christ and the Church," I pointed out. "Jesus Christ did not stay with the Father. He came to earth out of love for us and gave everything that He had to establish the relationship with us. Look, the Bible says you are to love your wife the way Christ loves the church. That means an active, pursuing love on your part."

I say to any husband who is trying to restore his marriage that he needs to understand that the only thing that will reach his estranged wife is a convincing, consistent demonstration that he really wants *her*. He is not trying to win her back because it is the right thing to do, or because it is best for the children, or because God is directing him this way. He needs to convince her that he wants her for himself. He has realized that the qualities she has are the ones he needs the most; he feels now that he is able to become the husband he ought to be; and he is eager for every opportunity to show her that he *can* and he *will* love her.

27

Notice that a husband must win his wife back by initiating love and pursuing, when necessary. A wife must win her husband back by responding with love at every opportunity. This is in keeping with the biblical roles and distinctive natures of husband and wife since the Creation.

The husband who has reason to believe his wife has been unfaithful should beware of asking her for information about the affair. It is enough to accept the fact that she has been indiscreet. The more you know, the more difficult it will be to handle it emotionally.

As Dr. Carlfred Broderick has noted, "In response to an informed spouse's assertion of the right to know 'everything,' repentant mates all too often supply details so vivid and concrete that they can scarcely be set aside."[5]

At the present time I am counseling two husbands, each of whom was determined to build a new love relationship with his wife after an episode of unfaithfulness on her part. But each made the crucial mistake of discussing the affair, probing for details, and they have since been tormented by the information they obtained.

As a general rule, there should be honesty between mates, and in answer to a direct question the affair must be admitted, but details should not be revealed. Tell your partner the subject is too painful to discuss and that you are much more interested in the love affair the two of you can have in your marriage. Unless you are asked, never confess an affair from the past that would come as a shock to your partner. Confession in this case is not virtuous honesty; it is a cruel act that puts the burden and pain on your mate. Keep the knowledge to yourself, confess your wrong to God and rest in His forgiveness.

In this extensive discussion of coping with adultery in marriage, I am in no way minimizing the sin of adultery or discounting the intense suffering it causes. But Christians should be the most realistic people in the world, enabled by the resources of Christ to confront and heal the deepest problems of human relationships. Some researchers say that more than 50 percent of Americans have committed adultery at some time in their marriage. From my vantage point as a family physician for twenty-five years, this estimate sounds quite conservative! But I want to emphasize that a one-time experience of adultery or even an affair of some duration need not destroy your marriage relationship. I can second Dr. Meier's observation that while the wounds from adultery run very deep, mature human beings have a tremendous capacity to forgive one another. Dr. Meier says, "Patients have told me that they never thought they would be able to forgive their mate if he or she ever committed adultery—until it actually happened. Then they were amazed at their own ability to forgive. They realized how much they wanted to restore intimate fellowship with their mate."[6]

So, when you must face the possibility of unfaithfulness on the part of your partner, remember that the Lord has grace enough for you, not only to endure or accept the situation, but also to redeem it.

2) Prepare to be "perfect," knowing you have a sufficiency of grace.

This may come as shocking information, but if you want to save your marriage, you cannot be just a "good" husband or wife. You have to be perfect in your behavior toward your partner. You must *do* and *be* everything the Bible prescribes for your role in marriage, and you must be very sensitive to avoid anything that will set your partner off. The least slip in word or action will give your mate the excuse he or she is looking for to give up on the marriage. Since resentment and rationalization are two of the key issues in the thinking of an unfaithful partner, even one remark spoken out of turn can fan the flames of old resentments and give weight to rationalizations that the partner is manufacturing to excuse his or her behavior.

One wife said, "I had to prove over a period of time that I had changed before my husband could believe it. He kept expecting to face my anger or a miserable silence when he walked in the door. For years, I was so moody, he never knew how he would find me. But now he is beginning to realize a new pattern has formed and things are not the way they used to be."

In talking about "perfect" behavior, we must always recognize the fact that it is the Lord who makes this possible, providing the pattern, the purpose, and the power for fundamental change in our behavior and attitudes. One wife married to an alcoholic said, "I had tried for years to manipulate the situation and change my husband by my own efforts. By nature I am strong-willed and ready to fight for what I want. But I just gave up one day. I remember beginning to cry in the bathtub and praying, 'Lord, you know that I can't handle my own life. Just take over for me, because I have learned that I can't control *anything*.

"And that," she went on, "was the turning point for our marriage. For both of us! Change came slowly. But I had the opportunity to pour out my heart to my husband and tell him how much I needed to be loved and to be put first in his life. He really took me seriously. He had a new motivation to quit drinking. A friend took him to Alcoholics Anonymous, and he has not had a drink in the last seven years. He's again become the wonderful man that I married. I thank God every day for my husband's sobriety and dignity and the love and respect we have for one another now. But the Lord had to change *me* before it could happen."

Three rules should be followed as you learn to love your partner with a love that can save your marriage:

First, *consistently do everything you can to please your mate and meet his or her needs and desires.* Love your partner in such a way that it will be interpreted as love. Study what your partner needs. One wife said, "I used to work in my husband's business, and I thought I was really helping him—really impressing him with my wisdom and efficiency. After our marriage ran into deep trouble, I discovered that wasn't what he needed at all. Now I am staying at home and becoming what he needs—not a whirlwind worker, but a woman who quietly loves him and believes in his ability to handle things well."

Pleasing your partner involves action—sometimes drastic action. A striking example of this is the wife who had had endless fights with her husband over flying in their plane. He was an enthusiastic private pilot; she was terrified of flying. But when it came down to saving her marriage, she went alone to the airport and took flying lessons, trusting the Lord to remove her fears. Today she is a pilot too, and they have a better marriage than ever before. She says, "I have found that spiritual growth gives me the courage I need to change."

Second, *consistently show your mate the respect and honor commanded in Scripture whether your mate personally merits it or not.* I cannot overemphasize this. All of the scriptural admonitions concerning marriage are rooted in this one principle. Study the New Testament passages on this subject, particularly Ephesians 5, Colossians 3, and 1 Peter 3 as translated in the Amplified Bible and other modern English versions. The husband, whatever his behavior, is by position the head of the wife and is to be treated with respect at all times. The wife, whatever her behavior, as an equal heir of the grace of life, is to be given the place of highest honor and special privilege by

31

her husband. As someone has said, she is to be treated like a Ming vase instead of an old garbage can!

Third, *totally avoid criticism of your mate*. Accept whatever your partner is or is not doing without comment or histrionics. Do not even suggest a secret disapproval. Again, the New Testament provides an abundance of instruction. In Colossians 3, for example, we read:

> Clothe yourselves therefore . . . [by putting on behavior marked by] tenderhearted pity and mercy, kind feeling, a lowly opinion of yourselves, gentle ways, [and] patience—which is tireless, long-suffering and has the power to endure whatever comes, with good temper. Be gentle and forbearing with one another and, if one has a difference (a grievance or complaint) against another, readily pardoning each other; even as the Lord has freely forgiven you, so must you also [forgive]. And above all these [put on] love and enfold yourselves with the bond of perfectness—which binds everything together completely in ideal harmony. And let the peace (soul harmony which comes) from the Christ rule (act as umpire continually) in your hearts. . . . And be thankful—appreciative, giving praise to God always (Colossians 3:12–15 AMPLIFIED).

3) Prepare to be rejected, knowing you have a sufficiency of grace.

What about rejection while you are trying to carry out these principles of love? I can only say that Jesus Christ was perfect and He was rejected! We should not be surprised when it happens to us. But do not give up your efforts because of rejection. One husband told me how he had sent a Valentine's Day flower arrangement to his estranged wife with a card from himself and their little girl. When he came home from work that night, the flowers were on the front step waiting for him—returned in scorn. Later, when she called him at his business, he told her, "I just want you to know that I love you. The hatred you are throwing at me right now cannot change that. I've discovered since we separated that my love for you has much higher limits than I ever realized."

She was quite taken aback by the loving way he had responded to her rejection of his gift. She said, "But you wouldn't want to live with a woman who doesn't love you?"

He answered, "Honey, love is something that doesn't grow overnight, especially when it has been treated the way both of us have treated our relationship in the past. You can't buy love. You aren't born with it. It's something you work at and build together. We haven't even tried that yet."

A happy wife wrote me a note of thanks for my counsel which gave her the courage to stick with her marriage. She said, "One little thing you said to me meant so much. You said, 'So what if your husband doesn't tell you he loves you right now!' I knew you were right. It really wasn't that important." This wife found that putting up with a little rejection was worth it in the long run in order to have a revitalized marriage.

I have talked with many women who tell me that when they do not feel their husband's love, the Lord has a way of loving them that is almost tangible. "Like being in the sunshine, just feeling the warmth of His love," several wives agreed. A lovely young wife carried that a step further in her own trying situation. She said that it was often difficult dressing to go out for the evening with her husband because she knew in advance that he would not treat her the way she longed to be treated. So she developed the habit of thinking of the Lord Jesus as her friend and escort for the evening. "It helped me tremendously," she said. "I looked my best for Him, I behaved my best for Him, and I was constantly aware of His steadying presence with me!"

In summary, you need to give love to your mate biblically, emotionally, and physically whether you receive a response or not. This is altogether possible through *agape* love. One wife, whose husband was involved with another woman, said, "I tried to show him that my love for him did not depend on how he treated me. I still showed him physical affection. I said to him sometimes, 'I love you, no matter what you are doing right now, and I believe the Lord means for us to be together.' I sent him little cards with appropriate messages that expressed my caring while we were apart. And, do you know, when we reconciled, I found that he had saved every one of them!"

I asked some wives who had been through the experience to give me their list of do's and don'ts for any woman trying to save her marriage. Here are the excellent suggestions they compiled:

- There can be no growth in your relationship as long as there is doubt as to your commitment to your marriage. Make your commitment!
- When your husband withholds his love, trust the Lord to meet your emotional needs. He won't let you down!
- Give your husband honor, love, and biblical respect even though his actions do not deserve it. Give him warm acceptance no matter what. The more hopeless your situation is, the more your loving behavior is apt to be accepted as genuine.
- Don't try to reform your husband. Just love him.
- Live one day at a time.
- Don't try to do it on your own. The Lord is with you!
- Don't be bitter against anyone in the situation. Never turn your children against their father. Forgive!
- Don't ask family or friends to take sides against your husband.

- Don't discuss your intimate marriage problems. Don't give fuel to gossip. Confide in the Lord, your counselor, and perhaps a close Christian friend whom you can trust to keep silence.
- Choose your biblical counselor wisely. *Never* discuss your problems with a friend of the opposite sex.
- Spend as much time in the Word of God as possible.
- Concentrate on yourself, redeeming the mistakes you have made, and asking God to show you how to change, rather than concentrating on your partner's failures.
- Do not separate. Encourage your husband to stay in the home, no matter what.
- Do not give your husband a divorce. Do all in your power to delay or prevent it. If you must consult a lawyer, make it clear to the lawyer that it is only for your financial protection and that of your children. Find a Christian lawyer who will help you preserve your marriage.
- Spend your time with people who will encourage you in spiritual growth.
- Do not overcompensate with your children. They need your love and stability while their father is gone, but they still need discipline. It will be hard to build a new love relationship with your husband when he does come home if the children are out of control.
- Do not try to defend yourself from gossip or criticism. Keep your mouth shut. The Lord will fight for you and you will hold your peace.
- Remember that the most innocent thing you say will get twisted. Avoid loose talk and do not listen to tale-bearing.
- When you do anything (large or small) to pull the marriage apart, you are going against God's will. Let that be your guideline for all decisions.

- Don't expect your husband to change overnight when he does come back home.
- The hardest time may be when you are reconciled and you have a tendency to fall back into old habit patterns. Don't do it!
- Hope all things, believe all things, endure all things.

The Book of Hosea in the Old Testament gives us the ultimate pattern for a love without limits which eventually reunites husband and wife in spite of great obstacles. This holds particular meaning for the husband whose wife has left him for someone else. Read the following narrative account of the love story of Hosea and ask God to strengthen your own resolve through this retelling of His Word.

The Love Story of Hosea

(A first-person narrative expository dramatic sermon by Dr. John W. Reed, Associate Professor of Practical Theology, Dallas Theological Seminary. Used by permission)

I have been called the prophet of the broken heart, but I would rather be remembered as the prophet of love and hope. I am Hosea, prophet of God to Israel, my homeland.

Come with me to my home on the outskirts of Samaria. There beneath the oak tree is Gomer, my wife; I love her as I love my own life. You will learn to love her too. Sitting beside her is our son, Jezreel. He is eighteen now, handsome and strong—a young man with a heart for God. At Gomer's feet and looking up at her is Ruhamah, our daughter. Do you

36

see how her raven hair glistens? She is the image of her mother. She was sixteen just half a year ago. And then Ammi, her brother—fifteen and as warm and bubbling as the flowing brook that you hear in the background.

We are happy and at peace. It has not always been so.

I began my ministry as a prophet almost thirty years ago during the reign of Jeroboam II. Those were years of prosperity. The caravans that passed between Assyria and Egypt paid taxes into Jeroboam's treasury and sold their goods in our midst. But they also left their sons and daughters and their gods. These gods and the gods of the ancient Canaanites and of Jezebel have wooed the hearts of my people. Altars built for sin offerings have become places for sinning.

If you were to walk through my land today, you would see images and altars in all the green groves. My people have many sheep and cattle. Some think that Baal, the so-called fertility god, is the giver of lambs, of calves, and the fruit of the field. Every city has its high place where Baal is worshiped. There is a high place not far from here—you are never far from a high place in Israel in these days! Sometimes at night we hear the beat of the priest's music and the laughter of the sacred prostitutes. Last week a man and woman who live three houses from us sacrificed their infant son to Baal.

You may wonder how Jehovah's people could sink to such unholy ways. It is because the priests of God have departed from Him. They delight in the sins of the people; they lap it up and lick their lips for more. And thus it is "Like priests, like people." Because the priests are wicked, the people are too. Surely God will judge. My beautiful land is just a few short years from being crushed under the iron heel of the Assyrian military might.

Yes, thirty years ago God appointed me a prophet in Israel. My father, Beeri, and my honored mother had taught me early to fear Jehovah, the One true God of Israel. They taught me to hate the calf deity of the first Jeroboam. Daily we prayed. Daily we longed to return to the Temple in Jerusalem. Daily we sang the songs of David and hungered for the coming of Messiah.

My ministry has always been hard. The first ten years were the hot-blooded days of my twenties. My sermons were sermons of fire. My heart bled for my people. I was little heeded and generally scorned. When I was thirty-two, God stirred me and I spent many days in prayer and meditation. I felt lonely and in need of a companion.

The first frosts of fall had tinted the leaves when I went with my parents to visit the home of Diblaim. In the busy activity of my ministry I had not seen the family for several years. We were engaged in lively conversation when through the door swept a young woman, Gomer, the daughter of Diblaim. I remembered her as a pretty and somewhat spoiled child. But now she was a hauntingly beautiful woman. Her ivory face was framed in a wealth of raven black hair. I found myself fascinated by her striking beauty and had great difficulty in turning my eyes from her.

As we returned to our home that day, my father

and I talked of many things. Yet, in my mind hung the image of a raven-haired Israelite. My father's friendship with Diblaim flourished and often I journeyed with him to visit. I was strangely drawn to Gomer. Diblaim and my father talked incessantly. Then one day my father astounded me with the proposal, "Hosea, it is my desire that you should marry Gomer." I did not question that I loved Gomer. But something about her troubled me. As most young women of her time she had a love for expensive clothing, jewelry and cosmetics. That I accepted as part of her womanhood. But she seemed somehow to be experienced beyond her years in the ways of the world.

Yet, I loved her. It was my father's will that I should marry her. I knew that my burning love for Jehovah would win her from any wanton ways. God confirmed to me that indeed Gomer was His choice as well.

I wooed her with the passion of a prophet. God had given me the gift of poetry and I flooded Gomer with words of love.

She responded to my love. We stood together beneath the flower-strewn canopy of the Hebrew marriage altar and pledged eternal love to God and to each other. We listened together to the reading of God's laws of marriage. We heard the reminder that our marriage was a symbol of the marriage between Jehovah and Israel, His wife.

I took Gomer to my home. We read together the Song of Songs which is Solomon's. We ate the sweet fruit of its garden of love. She was as refreshing to me as the first fig of the season. Gomer seemed

39

content in the love of God and of Hosea. I looked forward to the future with hope.

Shortly after the anniversary of our first year of marriage Gomer presented me with a son. I sought God's face and learned that his name was to be Jezreel—a name that would constantly remind Israel that God's judgment was surely coming. It was a stark reminder to me of the times in which we lived.

With the birth of Jezreel, Gomer seemed to change. She became distant and a sensual look flashed in her eye. I thought it a reaction to the responsibility of caring for our son. Those were busy days. The message of God inflamed me and I cried out throughout the land.

Gomer was soon with child again. This time a daughter was born. I learned from God that she was to be named Lo-Ruhamah. It was a strange name and troubled me deeply for it meant, "Not loved." For God said, "I will no longer show my love to the nation of Israel, that I should forgive her."

Gomer began to drift from me after that. Often she would leave after putting the children to bed and not return until dawn. She grew worn, haggard, and rebellious. I sought every way possible to restore her to me, but to no avail. About eighteen months later a third child was born, a boy. God told me to call him, Lo-Ammi—meaning, "Not my people." God said to Israel, "You are not my people, and I am not your God." In my heart a thorn was driven. I knew that he was not my son and that his sister was not the fruit of my love. Those were days of deep despair. I could not sing the songs of David. My heart broke within me.

After Lo-Ammi was weaned, Gomer drifted beyond my reach—and did not return. I became both father and mother to the three children.

I felt a blight upon my soul. My ministry seemed paralyzed by the waywardness of my wife. My prayers seemed to sink downward. But then Jehovah stirred me. I came to know that God was going to use my experience as an illustration of His love for Israel.

Love flamed again for Gomer and I knew that I could not give her up. I sought her throughout Samaria. I found her in the ramshackle house of a lustful, dissolute Israelite who lacked the means to support her. I begged her to return. She spurned all my pleadings. Heavy-hearted, I returned to the children and mourned and prayed. My mind warmed with a plan. I went to the market, bought food and clothes for Gomer. I bought the jewelry and the cosmetics she loved so dearly. Then I sought out her lover in private. He was suspicious, thinking that I had come to do him harm. When I told him my plan, a sly smile crept over his face. If I could not take Gomer home, my love would not let me see her wanting. I would provide all her needs and she could think that they came from him. We struck hands on the bargain. He struggled home under his load of provisions. I followed in the shadows.

She met him with joy and showered him with love. She told him to wait outside the house while she replaced her dirty, worn apparel with the new. After what seemed hours, she reappeared dressed in radiant splendor, like the Gomer I saw that first day at the home of her father. Her lover approached to embrace her, but she held him off. I heard her say, "No, surely the clothes and food and cosmetics are not from your hand but from the hand of Baal who gives all such things. I am resolved to express my gratitude to Baal by serving as a priestess at the high place."

It was as if I were suddenly encased in stone. I could not move. I saw her walk away. She seemed like the rebellious heifer I had seen as a youth in my father's herd. She could not be helped but would go astray. The more I tried to restore her the further she went from me. Feeble with inner pain, I stumbled home to sleepless nights and days of confusion and grief.

Gomer gave herself with reckless abandonment to the requirements of her role of priestess of Baal. She eagerly prostituted her body to the wanton will of the worshipers of the sordid deity.

My ministry became a pilgrimage of pain. I became an object of derision. It seemed that the penalty for the sin of Gomer—and of all my people— had settled upon me.

I fell back upon Jehovah. My father and mother helped me in the care and instruction of the three children. They responded in love and obedience. They became the Balm of Gilead for my wounded heart. The years passed as I sounded the burden of God throughout the land. Daily I prayed for Gomer and as I prayed love sang in my soul.

She was my nightly dream and so real that upon waking I often felt as if she had just left me again.

The years flowed on but the priests of Baal held her in their deadly clutch.

It was just over a year ago that it happened. The blush of spring was beginning to touch our land. In the midst of my morning hour of meditation, God seemed to move me to go among the people of Samaria. I was stirred with a sense of deep anticipation. I wandered through the streets.

Soon I was standing in the slave market. It was a place I loathed. Then I saw a priest of Baal lead a woman to the slave block. My heart stood still. It was Gomer. A terrible sight she was to be sure, but it was Gomer. Stark naked she stood on the block. But no man stared in lust. She was broken, haggard; and thin as a wisp of smoke. Her ribs stood out beneath the skin. Her hair was matted and touched with streaks of gray and in her eye was the flash of madness. I wept.

Then softly the voice of God's love whispered to my heart. I paused, confused. The bidding reached thirteen shekels of silver before I fully understood God's purposes. I bid fifteen shekels of silver. There was a pause. A voice on the edge of the crowd said, "Fifteen shekels and an homer of barley."

"Fifteen shekels, an homer and half of barley," I cried. The bidding was done.

As I mounted the slave block, a murmur of disbelief surged through the crowd. They knew me and they knew Gomer. They leaned forward in anticipation. Surely I would strike her dead on the spot for her waywardness. But my heart flowed with love.

I stood in front of Gomer and cried out to the people. "God says to you, 'Unless Israel remove her adulteries from her, I will strip her as naked as the day that she was born. I will make her like a desert

43

and leave her like a parched land to die of thirst.' "

I cried to a merchant at a nearby booth, "Bring that white robe on the end of the rack."

I paid him the price he asked. Then I tenderly drew the robe around Gomer's emaciated body and said to her, "Gomer, you are mine by the natural right of a husband. Now you are also mine because I have bought you for a price. You will no longer wander from me or play the harlot. You must be confined for a time and then I will restore you to the full joys of womanhood."

She sighed and fainting fell into my arms. I held her and spoke to my people, "Israel will remain many days without king or prince, without sacrifice or ephod. Afterward Israel will return and seek the Lord her God and David her king. She will come trembling to the Lord and to his benefits in the last days. And where it was said of Israel, 'Lo-Ruhamah—you are not loved, it will be said Ruhamah—you are loved.' For the love of God will not give you up, but pursue you down your days. And where Israel was called, 'Lo-Ammi, you are not my people,' it will be said, 'Ammi, you are the people of the living God,' for I will forgive you and restore you."

I returned home with my frail burden. I nursed Gomer back to health. Daily I read to her the writings of God. I taught her to sing the penitential song of David and then together we sang the songs of David's joyful praise to God. In the midst of song I restored her to God, to our home, to our children.

Do you not see how beautiful she is? I have loved her always, even in the depth of her waywardness because my God loved her. Gomer responded to God's love and to mine. She does not call me "my master" but "my husband." And the name of Baal has never again been on her lips.

Now my people listen to my message with new responsiveness for I am a prophet that has been thrilled with a great truth. I have come to know in the depth of my being how desperately God loves sinners. How deliberately He seeks them! How devotedly He woos them to Himself!

2

Resources for Change

Lovers never seem to tire of sharing tender reminiscences about their love affair: the intrigue of first meeting . . . the sweet moment when they confessed their caring . . . the thrill of their surrender to each other.

Intimate conversations of this nature are recorded in Scripture in the Song of Solomon. For example, when Shulamith and her beloved husband are vacationing in the countryside, Shulamith says, "Do you remember where our love began? Under the legendary sweetheart tree, of course, where every love begins and grows . . . Neither did our love begin without the pain, the fruitful pain of birth. . . ."

Of course, such reminiscences lead to a quickened desire for physical expression of their love: "O, my darling lover, make me your most precious possession held securely in your arms, held close to your heart," Shulamith whispers.

But the lovers are irresistibly drawn to speak of the quality of the love they share: its strength and its ultimate source. "True love is as strong and irreversible as the onward march of death," Shulamith says. "True love never ceases to care, and it would no more give up the beloved than the grave would give up the dead. *The fires of true love can never be quenched because the source of its flame is God himself.*"

These are the fires that I pray will be set ablaze in your own marriage!

My personal message to you in these pages has been that you and your mate do not have to live together in boredom or separate in misery. The alternative: to become *lovers* through the resources of what I will call *ultimate* love. This is what I would have you focus on in this chapter.

In marriage, the delights of all the human loves are mingled and made fragrant as a garden when ultimate love permeates the relationship. Even more important, the human loves are stabilized by the abiding presence of ultimate love. Feelings are momentary; ultimate love is lasting. The emotions of love are like those of other natural energies, always ebbing and flowing, even as the metabolic rate of the body incessantly changes, or the wind rises and falls. No passion endures on a consistent level. But your experience of love can be so reinforced by the tensiled strength of ultimate love that you will keep on loving and continue growing in love, no matter what your marriage must face in the course of a lifetime.

The Bible teaches (and in honesty we must agree) that we cannot save ourselves by any method: the Son of God had to become the Man Jesus, to live a perfect life, die for our sins, and live again in order to save us. Equally so, we cannot truly love by our own efforts. Again, God who is Love intervenes by giving us the priceless gift of ultimate love to be poured out to others.

Your own marriage partner should be the first, last, and in-between recipient of ultimate love. It is this that will save, restore, transform, and bless your marriage beyond your highest hopes.

How is this love expressed in human relationships—this love beyond which there is no other? We have described its qualities in other chapters, but let us take one more look from a different perspective. We can search out love's characteristic behavior by reading the letters the apostles wrote to believers of the early church. For example, if we read 2 Corinthians 12 we will find these qualities of love shining through the pages, and these are the very attitudes and actions that should be pervading our own marriage:

- Ultimate love pursues the beloved. It is a love of action that perseveres against great odds and never gives up. "I come to you," Paul writes.
- Ultimate love is unselfish—undemanding and compassionate. "I will not be a burden to you," Paul says.
- Ultimate love values the beloved. "I do not seek what is yours, but *you*," Paul reassures.
- Ultimate love freely assumes responsibility for the welfare of the beloved. "I am responsible for you," Paul states.
- Ultimate love gives to the limit without totaling the cost. "I will gladly spend and be expended for you," Paul affirms.
- Ultimate love grows in expression and does not diminish, regardless of the nature of the response. "I will love you the more," says Paul.
- Ultimate love is pure in motive and action, unadulterated by self-centered considerations. "I will not take advantage of you," Paul promises. "I will not exploit you. Everything I do is for your strengthening and building up."

Surely this love is fitted for the hard realities of life! When two people love this way, their marriage is touched by heaven despite the earthly problems from which no people are exempt.

Do you want to love and be loved like this? God is the only source of ultimate love; His is the power supply that feeds the fires of true love between husband and wife. It will not be enough to learn *about* God and this love. You must learn *from*

Him and become linked to Him in an eternal relationship through new life in Jesus Christ.

Let me explain how this occurs. Romans 10:9–10 says, "If thou shalt confess with thy mouth the Lord Jesus, and shalt believe in thine heart that God hath raised him from the dead, thou shalt be saved. For with the heart man believeth unto righteousness; and with the mouth confession is made unto salvation."

The Bible teaches that the Lord Jesus Christ is the Son of God who came to earth through the miracle of the virgin birth. He lived a perfect life as a man and, at a specific moment in history, He died on a cross to bear the sins of the whole world—the sins of every individual who will ever live. He died for you personally! Through that mighty act He paid the death penalty for sin and opened the way whereby your sins and mine can be forgiven and remembered no more.

After three days in the grave, Jesus demonstrated to all people for all time that He is God by rising from the dead—a legally authenticated fact of history. After more than a month spent on this earth in His resurrection body, He ascended to heaven with all power and authority in His possession. It is written in John 1:12: "But as many as received him, to them gave he power to become the sons of God, even to them that believe on his name."

Colossians 1:13–14 explains that the Father "hath delivered us from the power of darkness, and hath translated us into the kingdom of his dear Son: in whom we have redemption through his blood, even the forgiveness of sins."

Second Corinthians 5:17–18 promises that "Therefore if any man be in Christ, he is a new creature: old things are passed away; behold, all things are become new. And all things are of God, who hath reconciled us to himself by Jesus Christ. . . ."

Salvation and new life come through believing in Jesus Christ, the Son of God, as your Savior and receiving Him by faith. You must believe these things in your heart, then confess them with your mouth—both to God and to men.

Here is a prayer that you may wish to follow in expressing your faith in Jesus Christ as your Savior:

Heavenly Father, I realize I am a sinner and cannot do one thing to save myself. Right now I believe Jesus Christ died on the cross, shedding His blood as full payment for my sins—past, present, and future—and by rising from the dead He demonstrated that He is God. As best I know how, I am believing in Him, putting all my trust in Jesus Christ as my personal Savior, as my only hope for salvation and eternal life. Right now I am receiving Christ into my life, and I thank You for saving me as You promised, and I ask that You will give me increasing faith and wisdom and joy as I study and believe Your Word. For I ask this in Jesus' name. Amen.

When we put our trust in Jesus Christ and our lives link up with His, we become new people. Our problems may seem the same, but our ability to cope with them is all new. We have suspected that we needed to change. Now we can face it and draw on new resources to effect that change.

We as Christians have a source of love beyond ourselves. We have a sufficiency of grace for every situation. We have a new kind of strength—the power of the Lord Jesus Christ—that manifests itself through our own weakness. We now have the ability to behave in the ways that will bring order and blessing into our lives. It is now possible for us to apply every biblical principle concerning marriage and to resolve relationship problems with those closest to us.

As Christian psychiatrist Frank B. Minirth has observed, "Christian counseling is unique because it depends not only on man's willpower to be responsible, but also on God's enabling, indwelling power of the Holy Spirit to conquer man's problems. I do not wish to imply that man has no responsibility for his actions, for he does; and many Christians choose to act irresponsibly. However, our willingness and attempts to be responsible must be coupled with God's power. Through God's power, man need no longer be a slave to a weak will, his past environment, or social situations. Problems do not disappear when one accepts Christ, but there is a new power to deal with them."[1]

The chances are good that you have read this book through to the end because you are hungering for a change in your marriage. You have, no doubt, seen many areas of your life that cry out for improvement. And, by now, you have realized that change must occur within yourself before you can hope for your partner to change. You know for a certainty that running away from your problems will not cause change within. You can go a thousand miles away, start a new life, get a divorce, remarry, and you will still find yourself on the old emotional treadmill, facing compounded problems and an even greater need to change.

But if you have trusted Jesus Christ as your Savior, the answers are within your grasp. You do not have to run away from yourself or your problems any longer. The question now is not: *Can* I change? but *Will* I change?

No writer has made this point more clearly than Charles (Chuck) Swindoll, radio Bible teacher, in a column entitled "CAN'T OR WON'T?" He writes:

No offense, but some of you don't have any business reading this today. Normally, I do not restrict my column to any special group of people. But now I must. This time it is *for Christians only*. Everything I write from now to the end is strictly for the believer

51

in Christ. If you're not there yet, you can toss this aside because you lack a major ingredient: the power of God. Non-Christians are simply unable to choose righteous paths consistently. That divine response upon which the Christian can (and *must*) draw is not at the unbeliever's disposal. That is, not until personal faith in Jesus Christ is expressed.

But if you know the Lord, you are the recipient of limitless ability . . . incredible strength. Just read a few familiar lines out of the Book, *slowly* for a change:

> I can do all things through Him who strengthens me (Philippians 4:13).

> . . . "My grace is sufficient for you, for power is perfected in weakness." Most gladly, therefore, I will rather boast about my weaknesses, that the power of Christ may dwell in me (2 Corinthians 12:9).

> For this reason I bow my knees before the Father . . . that He would grant you, according to the riches of His glory, to be strengthened with power through His Spirit in the inner man (Ephesians 4:14, 16).

> . . . He has granted to us His precious and magnificent promises, in order that by them you might become partakers of the divine nature . . . (2 Peter 1:4).

And one more:

> No temptation has overtaken you but such as is common to man; and God is faithful, who will not

allow you to be tempted beyond what you are able, but with the temptation will provide the way of escape also, that you may be able to endure it (1 Corinthians 10:13).

Wait a minute now. Did you read every word—or did you skip a line or two? If so, please go back and *slowly* graze over those five statements written to you, a Christian. It's really important.

Okay, what thought stands out the most? Well, if someone asked me that question, I'd say, "special strength or an unusual ability from God." In these verses it's called several things: strength, power, divine nature, ability. God has somehow placed into the Christian's insides a special something, that extra inner reservoir of power that is more than a match for the stuff life throws at us. When in operation, phenomenal accomplishments are achieved, sometimes even *miraculous*.

Let's get specific.

It boils down to the choice of two common words in our vocabulary. Little words, but, oh, so different! "Can't" and "won't."

We prefer to use "can't."

"I just *can't* get along with my wife."
"My husband and I *can't* communicate."
"I *can't* discipline the kids like I should."
"I just *can't* give up the affair I'm having."
"I *can't* stop overeating."
"I *can't* find the time to pray."
"I *can't* quit gossiping."

No, any Christian who really takes those five passages we just looked at (there are dozens more) will have to confess the word really should be "won't." Why? Because we have been given the power, the ability to overcome. Literally! And therein lies hope in hoisting anchors that would otherwise hold us in the muck and mire of blame and self-pity.

One of the best books you can read this year on overcoming depression is a splendid work by two physicians, Minirth and Meier, appropriately entitled *Happiness Is a Choice*. These men agree:

> As psychiatrists we cringe whenever (Christian) patients use the word *can't*. . . . Any good psychiatrist knows that "I can't" and "I've tried" are merely lame excuses. We insist that our patients be honest with themselves and use language that expresses the reality of the situation. So we have our patients change their *can'ts* to *won'ts*. . . . If an individual changes all his *can'ts* to *won'ts,* he stops avoiding the truth, quits deceiving himself, and starts living in reality. . . .

What a difference one word makes!

> "I just *won't* get along with my wife."
> "My husband and I *won't* communicate."
> "I *won't* discipline the kids like I should."
> "I just *won't* give up the affair I'm having."
> "I *won't* stop overeating."
> "I *won't* find the time to pray."
> "I *won't* quit gossiping."

Non-Christians have every right and reason to use "can't," because they really can't! They are victims, trapped and bound like slaves in a fierce and endless struggle. Without Christ and His power, they lack what it takes to change permanently. They don't because they can't!

But people like us? Hey, let's face it, we don't because we won't . . . we disobey because we want to, not because we have to . . . because we choose to, not because we're forced to. The sooner we are willing to own up realistically to our responsibility and stop playing the blame game at pity parties for ourselves, the more we'll learn and change and the less we'll burn and blame.

Wish I could find a less offensive way to communicate all this, but I just can't.

Oops!

Chuck Swindoll
(used by permission)

Poet and hymn-writer Annie Johnson Flint expressed the same truth in words that countless Christians have sung with grateful hearts:

His love has no limits; His grace has no measure;
His power has no boundary known unto men.
For out of His infinite riches in Jesus,
He giveth, and giveth, and giveth again!

And so some crucial choices lie before us. We must choose first of all whether to become Christians and to be linked eternally with the God of love and the Lord of life. Then we must choose whether to use the great resources He makes available to every believer.

We also determine by action or inaction the quality of

love-life we will have in our marriage. It is vain to hope that a troubled relationship will get better on its own, or that somehow time will bring about more love, or that we will (accidentally?) draw closer to each other. It is up to each of us to build our house of love.

The Bible makes the choice clear in the Book of Proverbs. We are told, "The wise woman builds her house, but the foolish tears it down with her own hands" (Proverbs 14:1 NASB). "He that troubleth his own house shall inherit the wind . . ." (Proverbs 11:29) and will live to regret it.

But this need not be so! For, "By wisdom a house is built, and by understanding it is established; and by knowledge the rooms are filled with all precious and pleasant riches" (Proverbs 24:34 NASB). Our wisdom comes from a daily study of the Word of God, applying its counsel to the details of life and letting it shape our attitudes and behavior in every situation.

As you continue gathering biblical information on your role as husband or wife and learning how to love, and as learning is followed by doing, and principle by practice, you will find your obedience transformed into the passionate and joyous pleasure of loving your mate.

Isobel Kuhn in *Stones of Fire* quotes a phrase from Dr. G. Campbell Morgan that perfectly describes the uniqueness of the love-life that is available to every Christian couple:

> Principle shot through with passion,
> Passion held by principle.

This is the pattern we aim for. And as we aim we find 2 Chronicles 25:9 wonderfully true: Whatever plateau you have reached in your love-life, *"The LORD is able to give thee much more than this!"*

Notes

Chapter 1

[1]Paul D. Meier, *You Can Avoid Divorce* (Grand Rapids: Baker Book House, 1978), p. 4.

[2]Ibid., pp. 5–6.

[3]Anne Kristin Carroll, *From the Brink of Divorce* (Garden City, New York: A Doubleday-Galilee Original, 1978), p. 19.

[4]Gloria Okes Perkins, "Fly by the Instruments," *Good News Broadcaster* (October 1978): 26–27.

[5]Carlfred B. Broderick, "Guidelines for Preserving Fidelity," *Medical Aspects of Human Sexuality* (May 1980): 21.

[6]Meier, *You Can Avoid Divorce*, p. 8.

Chapter 2

[1]Frank B. Minirth, *Christian Psychiatry* (Old Tappan, New Jersey: Revell, 1977), pp. 31–32.

Suggested Reading

Adams, Jay E. *Christian Living in the Home* (Phillipsburg, New Jersey: Presbyterian and Reformed Publishing Company, 1972). A precise and powerful application of scriptural principles to the problems of today's home and family.

Augsburger, David W. *Seventy Times Seven: The Freedom of Forgiveness* (Chicago: Moody Press, 1970). A classic on the subject of forgiveness and resolving of hostility.

Brandt, Henry, with Landrum, Phil. *I Want My Marriage to Be Better* (Grand Rapids, Michigan: Zondervan Publishing House, 1976). A Christian psychologist explains how walls arise in marriage and shows how they can be removed.

Burkett, Larry. *Your Finances in Changing Times* (Campus Crusade for Christ, Inc., 1975). God's principles for managing money described by a Christian financial counselor. Recommended for every marriage.

Campbell, Ross, M.D. *How to Really Love Your Child* (Wheaton, Illinois: Victor Books, SP Publications Inc., 1977). Valuable instruction in how to love those closest to you with many applications to the husband-wife relationship.

Carroll, Anne Kristin. *Together Forever* (Grand Rapids: Zondervan Publishing House, 1982). Wise, sympathetic advice for the individual caught in a problem marriage. A must for those who want to save their marriage.

Cooper, Darien B. *You Can Be the Wife of a Happy Husband* (Wheaton, Illinois: Victor Books, SP Publications Inc., 1974). A helpful explanation of the wife's God-given role.

Dillow, Linda. *Creative Counterpart* (Nashville, Tennessee: Thomas Nelson, Inc., 1978). Good ideas for the Christian wife to implement.

Dobson, James. *What Wives Wish Their Husbands Knew About Women* (Wheaton, Illinois: Tyndale House Publishers, Inc., 1975). This popular book includes an important section on hormonal problems during menopause.

Fooshee, George and Marjean. *You Can Beat the Money Squeeze* (Old Tappan, New Jersey: Power Books, Fleming H. Revell Company, 1980). Practical principles of finance for the marriage of the '80s.

Glickman, S. Craig. *A Song for Lovers* (Downers Grove, Illinois: InterVarsity Press, 1976). Perceptive discussion of love in marriage based on the Song of Solomon.

LaHaye, Tim and Beverly. *The Act of Marriage* (Grand Rapids, Michigan: Zondervan Publishing House, 1976). Excellent suggestions for improving the sex relationship in any marriage.

Landorf, Joyce. *Tough and Tender* (Old Tappan, New Jersey: Fleming H. Revell Company, 1975). A sensitive consideration of husband and wife roles in marriage.

Lewis, C. S. *The Four Loves* (New York: Harcourt Brace Jovanovich, Inc., 1960). A refreshing view of the basic kinds of human love.

Mayhall, Jack and Carole. *Marriage Takes More Than Love* (Colorado Springs: NAVpress, 1978). Down-to-earth solutions for marital conflicts.

Meredith, Don. *Becoming One* (Nashville, Tennessee: Thomas Nelson Publishers, 1979). Realistic suggestions for a successful marriage.

Merrill, Dean. *How to Really Love Your Wife* (Grand Rapids: Zondervan Publishing House, 1980). A thought-provoking job description for the married man.

Miles, Herbert J. *Sexual Happiness in Marriage* (Grand Rapids, Michigan: Zondervan Publishing House, 1967). Written by a pioneer in the field of sex in marriage from the biblical viewpoint.

Minirth, Frank B., M.D. *Christian Psychiatry* (Old Tappan, New Jersey: Fleming H. Revell Company, 1977). A balanced, biblical approach to personal problems.

Minirth, Frank B., M.D., and Meier, Paul D., M.D. *Happiness Is a Choice*. (Grand Rapids: Baker Book House, 1978). Two Christian psychiatrists explain how to conquer depression and establish a sense of well-being.

Powell, John. *Why Am I Afraid to Love?* (Niles, Illinois: Argus Communications Co., Revised, 1972). A sensitive discussion of the barriers that hinder loving and how to overcome them.

Rice, Shirley. *Physical Unity in Marriage* (Norfolk, Virginia: The Tabernacle Church of Norfolk, 1973). An excellent treatment of the subject from the wife's view.

Short, Ray E. *Sex, Love, or Infatuation* (Minneapolis: Augsburg Publishing House, 1978). A good overview of genuine love as it should be experienced in marriage.

Strauss, Richard L. *Marriage Is for Love* (Wheaton, Illinois: Tyndale House Publishers, 1973). How to make your marriage work by applying God's principles.

Swindoll, Charles R. *Killing Giants, Pulling Thorns* (Portland, Oregon: Multnomah Press, 1978). Strong encouragement, biblical teaching in exciting language. Tells how to deal with the giants and thorns in your own life.

Timmons, Tim. *One Plus One* (Washington, D.C.: Canon Press, 1974). A detailed look at the scriptural plan for oneness in marriage.

Trobisch, Ingrid. *The Joy of Being a Woman* (New York: Harper & Row Publishers, 1975). A guidebook to the Christian woman's own body and spirit.

Trobisch, Walter. *I Married You* (New York: Harper & Row Publishers, 1971). A creative, compassionate approach to the meaning of marriage based upon the author's insight as a counselor and as a husband.

Wessel, Helen. *The Joy of Natural Childbirth* (San Francisco: Harper & Row Publishers, 1973). A useful book for those considering natural childbirth, written from a Christian perspective.

Wheat, Ed, M.D., and Gaye. *Intended for Pleasure* (Old Tappan, New Jersey: Fleming H. Revell Company, 1977). Sexual fulfillment in Christian marriage clearly and sensitively explained from the medical, emotional, and spiritual perspectives. Indexed and illustrated.

Wright, H. Norman. *Communication: Key to Your Marriage* (Glendale, California: G/L Publications, 1974). Good ideas for the husband and wife who want to enrich their marriage through better communication.

Recommended Cassettes

These may be obtained from your local Christian bookstore or ordered from Bible Believers Cassettes, Inc., 130 Spring St., Springdale, AR 72764. BBC, Inc., is the world's largest *free loan* library of Bible study cassettes with more than ten thousand different teaching cassettes for loan. More than one thousand of these are on marriage and the family. Write for further information.

Burkett, Larry. *Christian Financial Concepts, God's Principles of Handling Money*. An album set: six cassettes, one workbook.

Painter, Alice. *The Challenge of Being a Woman*. A Bible study course including twelve cassettes, one workbook.

Wheat, Ed, M.D. *Sex Technique & Sex Problems in Marriage*. Three hours of intimate counsel to enrich your marriage by a Christian family doctor who is also a certified sex therapist. Two-cassette album.

Wheat, Ed, M.D. *Love-Life for Every Married Couple*. Listening together to this two-cassette album will improve your verbal communication regarding your love relationship. Three hours of positive counsel to enhance your marriage.